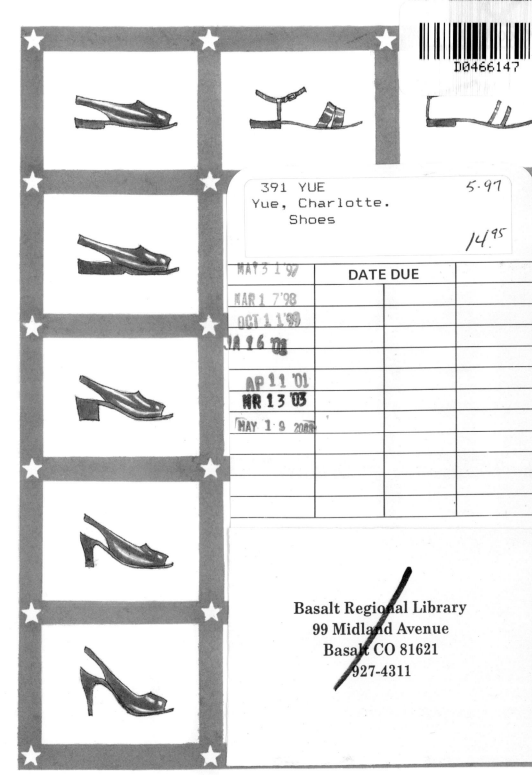

MAY 3 1 '97	DATE DUE	
MAR 1 7 '98		
OCT 1 1 '99		
JA 1 6 '01		
AP 11 '01		
MR 13 '03		
MAY 1 9 2008		

SHOES

THEIR HISTORY
IN WORDS AND PICTURES

Charlotte and David Yue

Houghton Mifflin Company
Boston   1997

To Tsing-Ying Tsang Lim,
a remarkable person
and a fashion inspiration

For information about this and other Houghton Mifflin
trade and reference books and multimedia products,
visit The Bookstore at Houghton Mifflin on the
World Wide Web at http://www.hmco.com/trade/.

Manufactured in the United States of America
The text of this book is set in 14 point Dante
VB 10 9 8 7 6 5 4 3 2 1

Library of Congress Cataloging-in-Publication Data

Yue, Charlotte.
Shoes/by Charlotte and David Yue.
p. cm.
Includes bibliographical references (p.   ).
Summary: Relates the history and lore of many
of the kinds of shoes worn by men, women, and
children throughout the world.
ISBN 0–395–72667–0
1. Shoes — History — Juvenile literature.
[1. Shoes.]   I. Yue, David.   II. Title.
TT678.5Y84   1997
391'.413 — dc20   96–17220   CIP   AC

Contents

1.
What Do Your Shoes Say About You?

How did you choose the shoes you are wearing today? Did you slide into your most comfortable ones? Did you select them to go with the outfit you are wearing? Do you have plans that require special shoes? Did weather conditions influence your choice? Did you put on the same kind of shoes that your friends would be wearing or did you choose a pair that made you feel different and unique? Were you making a fashion statement or a political statement with your choice? Do your shoes express your mood? Do you plan to wear the same shoes all day, or change them later on? How about tomorrow?

Shoes tell a lot about their wearer. Sometimes they give clues about what the person is going to do. We recognize the shoes of a ballet dancer, a tap dancer, a runner, a cowboy, a soccer player, a construction worker, a nurse, a firefighter, a fisherman. We can make guesses about the personality of the wearer — a sensible person, an active person, one who likes to be fashionable, different, or comfortable. Shoes might tell us whether the wearer is wealthy. Sherlock Holmes could judge a man's occupation by his boots.

We could make an estimate of a person's height by the size of his shoes. If we examined how the shoes have changed shape with wear and the places where they are most worn out, the shoes might tell us something about the wearer's foot structure and how he walks and stands.

Of course, we can easily be deceived by all these clues. Shoes that were originally made for special purposes frequently have been adopted by people who found them fashionable, comfortable, or useful for a different purpose. Shoe fashions are borrowed from all times and places. Men and women adapt fashion ideas from each other. Shoes are not always made specifically for left and right feet; some shoes can be worn on either foot. People sometimes force their feet into tiny shoes to make the feet seem smaller, and clowns wear huge shoes to look funny. Special pads in shoes can adjust irregularities in foot structure so that shoes wear out normally.

Almost as soon as people first started protecting their feet with shoes, they began to experiment with techniques and materials to make shoes that fit well and suited their needs. They wanted shoes for the same reasons we do today. Shoes could make the wearers look special and could help them do their jobs safely. They devised footwear for traveling through mud and snow and set aside shoes for special occasions and ceremonies. Sometimes people have worn shoes to identify themselves with a particular group. Since early times people have wanted beauty in their lives and have needed to express their individuality and, for these reasons, have created shoes of different styles and materials.

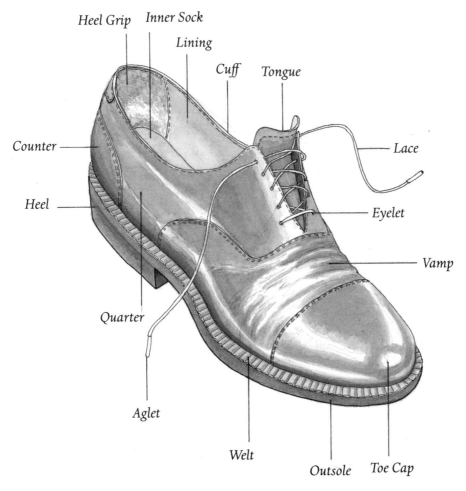

Shoe Parts

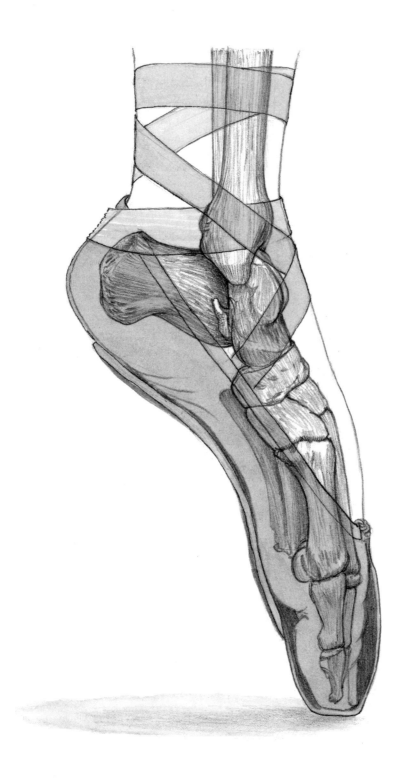

2.
Two Feet, No Feathers

Walking on two feet, without feathers, has been used as a definition of what makes us human since the time of the ancient Greeks, and most scientists still agree that bipedalism is one of the crucial factors separating humans from other animals.

The human body underwent many adaptations that made upright walking possible. We have a broad pelvis, large leg bones, and amazing feet. Feet are well adapted for getting us around on rough, rocky, powdery, or uneven ground. Our feet carry us uphill and downhill. We walk, run, jump, hop, dance, swim, hike, or just stand still with the help of our feet.

The foot is small, but considering all the movements it must make, it is complex. Each foot has twenty-eight bones and thirty-

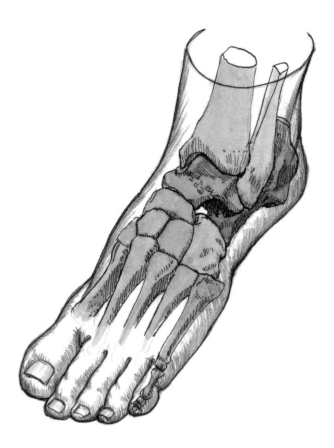

two joints covered with gristly cartilage and bound together by tough ligaments, which are supported by elastic muscles and anchored to the bones by strong tendons. Muscles produce movement when they contract and pull on their connected tendons, which move the bones and joints in response to messages carried by delicate nerves. A system of blood vessels nourishes and repairs the bones, muscles, skin, and tissues of the feet and regulates their temperature.

The feet account for only about two percent of our total body weight, but those two small structures support the weight of our whole body when we stand. They are shock absorbers that cushion the forces that crash down on them when we walk, run, or jump. Our feet are levers that propel our bodies forward when we move. When our feet push off from the ground, they need to be rigid; but they need to be flexible when they hit the ground to absorb the shock and adjust to the terrain. The design of the foot includes three arches that help absorb shock, balance the body, and create the lever that moves us along. By raising and lowering the arches, feet can get longer, wider, shorter, narrower, and adjust for all the movements we expect of them. All these changing dimensions of the foot must fit into a shoe that has only one shape and size.

Feet suffer a lot of wear and tear. An average person walks 15,000 steps a day. To withstand the punishment we inflict on our feet every day, the skin of the sole of the foot is ten times thicker than the skin on the rest of our bodies. Extremely sensitive for something so tough and thick, the sole can feel a feather brushing against it. Feet need to be sensitive to help us adjust our stride and speed as we negotiate different surfaces. If you've ever tried walking when your foot has fallen asleep, you will know how essential the feeling in your foot is.

Some people even think that there are reflex areas in the feet that correspond to all the major organs and all parts of the body. They believe that because the foot is so sensitive, it is possible to relieve problems anywhere in the body by massaging the area of the foot linked with the part that is giving them trouble. In any case, a good foot massage is relaxing and makes most people feel somewhat better. Sore feet definitely affect the way we feel. We literally can't get far without healthy feet.

3.
Humans Invent Shoes

Although our feet are well designed for a variety of movements, they cannot always give enough protection from burning sands, intense cold, and very rough surfaces. The first shoe designs depended on where the inventor lived, the conditions people there needed protection from, and the materials available. Being able to move fast was important for survival. Shoes needed to be lightweight but still strong enough for adequate protection. They needed to enclose the foot and not easily come loose.

In warm climates, early people found or made flat pieces of material that they could tie onto the soles of their feet. People in colder climates wrapped animal skins around their feet and legs and tied them on with thongs. In some places a short bag-like cover that only enclosed the foot was worn. So from early times, humans had three basic types of footwear — the sandal, the boot, and the shoe.

How do we know what shoes people wore? Some actual examples exist, and we can also learn about them from paintings and sculptures. Sometimes footwear is described in writings or listed in inventories. Although we know about general styles, it is often difficult to figure out exactly how a particular shoe was made.

The oldest shoes that have been found date back about ten thousand years. They were discovered in a cave in Oregon, preserved under layers of pumice and volcanic ash. To make the sole, grass and shredded sagebrush bark were twisted into ropes about as thick as a pencil. Five pieces of this rope, somewhat longer than the foot, were laid out lengthwise. These were woven tightly together with thinner rope, leaving loops on the sides as the rope was interlaced back and forth. The front ends of the five strands were folded back over the foot to protect the toes. This "sandal" was held on by a tie string drawn through the side loops. Rabbit fur and pine needles were sometimes added for padding and extra warmth.

Probably by the late Stone Age, around 6500 B.C., people had developed the basic skills for preparing animal hides and sewing them together to make shoes.

It was not long before shoes became more than just necessities and were used to set the wearer apart from other people. Through-

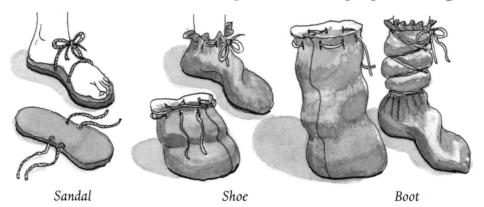

Sandal   Shoe   Boot

out history, shoes have been worn as symbols of religion, rank, wealth, or power. Decoration, color, and style became as important as workmanship and fit. Whenever people traveled to other places, traded with other groups, or conquered other lands, shoe inventions and fashions were exchanged.

Early man made his own shoes, and some people continued to make shoes for themselves and their families until recent times. Shoemaking, however, soon became a job that everyone who could afford to left to skilled workers.

Until the last couple of centuries, the design of men's shoes was given more attention than those for women. Women's feet were often hidden beneath long skirts. Men had a greater variety of styles and ornaments; women usually wore shoes of more delicate materials. Working people needed sturdy, practical footwear. Wealthy people wore shoes that showed they didn't need to work, and in some cases, even to walk. Children have usually worn smaller versions of adult styles.

Oldest Known Shoe — Oregon Sandal

In ancient Egypt, shoes were at first a status symbol, worn only by nobles, priests, and warriors. Those who wore shoes protected their feet from the hot sands with sandals, which were easy to put on and take off and kept feet cool and well ventilated. Egyptian sandals were often just a sole, held on by a thong that passed between the big toe and the second toe and was attached to a band that went around the ankle or instep.

These sandals were usually woven from plant fibers like papyrus, flax, or palm. The Egyptians also knew how to tan and dress hides to make leather. Sometimes they made soles of two thicknesses, sewing a heavy leather sole to a thin upper sole. They used waxed thread for sewing, as well as circular knives, awls, and other tools similar to those still used by modern shoemakers. Shoes were shaped to fit right and left feet and were dyed scarlet, green, and purple and ornamented with jewels and gold. Pharaohs' shoes were works of art.

Later Egyptians adopted new shoe styles brought back by travelers, traders, and warriors — shoes with upturned toes, sock-like boots, and low slippers. They invented footwear for special jobs. Butchers wore shoes with heels to raise their feet off the bloody, slippery ground when they were slaughtering animals. Shoes some-

Egyptian Sandal

times had a linen lining with a figure of a bound captive painted on it, so that warriors could symbolically crush their enemies beneath their feet. By around 1300 B.C., more people were wearing shoes. It had become improper to go barefoot outside and no upper class man or woman appeared barefoot in the streets.

In Egypt, other parts of Africa, and many Asian cultures, the same basic shoe styles have been worn for thousands of years. Even today, when American sneakers and other western-style shoes are available in most parts of the world, these traditional shoes are still being made.

Sumerians, Assyrians, and Babylonians, who lived in the fertile land between the Tigris and Euphrates rivers in what is now part of Iraq, wore sandals with leather soles, loops for the big toe, and a heel guard for protection from mud and rain. They also wore shoes with turned-up toes and pointed toes. When they were at home, Sumerian and Babylonian women wore "mules," an early version of the backless slippers worn today. Warriors and hunters had soft boots laced in front, a style that became known as "buskins." Some military boots were completely covered with painting or embroidery. Sometimes soldiers just wore sandals with bronze or brass leg protectors called "greaves."

Assyrian Sandal

Babylonians were famous for the fine leather they made from kid or goatskin tanned with sumac and dyed a deep red color. The secret method was preserved through the centuries and eventually brought to Europe by the Moors when they invaded Spain. The leather was produced in Cordova, a city in Spain, and became popular throughout Europe in the Middle Ages. It was known as "cordovan" and the shoes made from it were called "Babylonian shoes."

Babylonians also made shoes of felt, cloth, and wood. Sometimes they made shoes from strips of different colored leathers. They liked perfumed leather and often attached small metal trinkets to their shoes, so that they could enjoy their sound as they walked.

In India people wore sandals made of straw, grass, rope, and wood. From early times they traded with Egypt and the Near East, and shoe styles were passed along the trade routes. They liked a sandal that was held on by a large knob gripped between the big toe and the second toe. Trade with India brought these knob sandals to Africa, where they are still popular today. Cows are sacred to the Hindus, so there were few leather shoes in India. Instead, Indians wore mules, slippers, and boots made from felt and velvet, frequently decorated with exquisite embroidery. They have usually preferred shoes with curved and pointed toes. Their riding boots often had an iron heel to grip the stirrup.

In a large country like China, people have worn many different kinds of foot protection, depending on what materials were available and the conditions of their particular area. Some people wear shoes made from twisted rice stalks or rope sandals with a wooden sole. In parts of China where the climate is harsh, the people wear

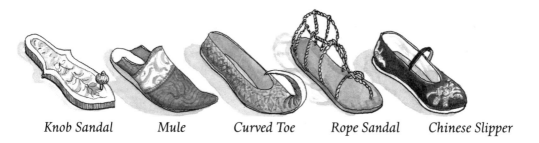

Knob Sandal   Mule   Curved Toe   Rope Sandal   Chinese Slipper

felt or fur-lined leather boots, often very colorful and richly ornamented with embroidery and appliqué. Slippers of felt, silk, velvet,
cotton, or woven rush are fashionable in more moderate climates.

Public officials wore black satin boots with white felt soles. They
liked wide tops on their boots so they could store papers, a pipe, or
perhaps a fan in them. In rainy weather people wore mud shoes
with high wooden soles that looked like tapered pedestals.

The Chinese found small feet very beautiful and developed one
of the most extreme customs for keeping feet tiny. According to
some accounts, the practice began in the eleventh century B.C.
when an empress who was born with club feet declared small feet
the height of beauty and ordered her courtiers to imitate her tiny,
deformed feet. Most authorities believe this custom began much
later, in the first part of the tenth century A.D., and was a fashion
based on popular court dancing girls who performed on tiptoe.

Buskin   Indian Riding Boot   Chinese Boot   Black Satin Boot   Pedestal Shoe

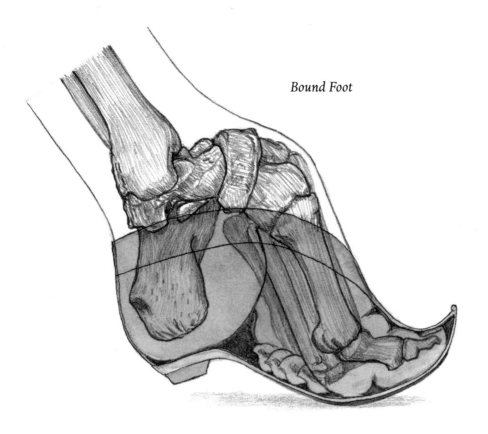

Bound Foot

The feet of very young girls from wealthy families were tightly bound with the toes bent under. The front part of the foot and the heel were forced together. Eventually the girl's foot hardened into a distorted structure about four inches long and she would never be able to walk normally. She hobbled slowly in what was called the "willow walk," which was considered very beautiful, especially by Chinese men. Women wore lavishly decorated miniature shoes which they made themselves. Tiny "lily feet," as they were called, were considered sexy, stylish, and an important status symbol. Bound feet showed that the girl's family was so wealthy she didn't have to do any physical labor and always needed to be waited on. Mothers bound their daughters' feet in the belief that they would be more likely to have wealthy husbands and good homes. Early attempts to ban the custom were ignored. The practice was finally outlawed in 1912.

Centuries ago, the Japanese developed the classic shoe styles that are still being worn today. Although men and women wear the same styles, men's shoes are usually rectangular and women's have rounded edges. They have a flat sandal, called a *"zori,"* which is held to the foot by two straps that pass between the first two toes. The sole is made of plaited hemp or felt. It has long been the custom in Japan to go shoeless indoors, but sometimes they wear a white cotton mitten for their feet, called a *"tabi,"* which has a thick sole and a separate section for the big toe and fastens up the back with hooks or snaps. Most often it is worn outdoors with the *zori* or with the *"geta,"* a thong shoe similar to the *zori,* but with a wooden sole from two to six inches high. Nobles wore *getas* that were ten to twelve inches high to raise themselves above the common people.

Early civilizations developed many of the shoe styles and shoe-making techniques still known today. Humans were showing their practical inventiveness at designing well-fitted shoes that solved particular problems with ingenuity, as well as their artistic abilities at creating beautiful shoes. And, since the earliest civilizations, shoes have demonstrated what foolish things humans are willing to do for fashion and beauty.

Tabi   *Zori*   *Geta*

4.
Classical Shoes

Early Greeks went barefoot, but when they wanted more protection for their feet, they wore a simple, unconfining sandal that they called a *"pedila."* Common people had sandals with wooden soles that fit either foot. They also wore a shoe called a *"carbatina,"* which was made from a single piece of rawhide with holes punched along the edge. A cord was threaded through the holes and tied, drawing the edges together. The *carbatina* was similar to the moccasins of Native Americans. Wealthier people wore sandals with leather or felt soles cut for right and left feet. The sandals of aristocrats were higher, with thicker soles made with layers of cork.

For early Greeks, simplicity was the essential element for shoe design. Later, craftsmanship became more elegant and materials

Roman Crepida with Lingula

more luxurious. The quality of the decoration, the strap arrangement, and the design of individual sandals became more important. Shoe fashions changed with the times, and different styles were worn for specific occasions.

In ancient Greece, shoemakers used division of labor to produce shoes. Some workers cut out the leather, and others attached soles. Usually separate shops made men's shoes and women's shoes. A few shops sold ready-to-wear sandals.

The *"krepis"* was the fashionable shoe of fourth century B.C. It was a variation on the *pedila* or sandal. It had a thick sole, leather at the sides and back, and a tongue, or *"lingula,"* which folded over the instep and covered the straps. It was worn by men and women, civilians and soldiers, and was often portrayed on the feet of gods and heroes. Shoes were distinguished by the ornamentation of the tongue. On the shoes of rich or important people, or on those intended for special occasions, the *lingula* was often elaborately decorated or made entirely of gold, silver, or ivory. The *krepis* of the military sometimes added a leg protection called a *"cnemis."*

Greeks also wore many kinds of boots. An early style was made from untanned leather with the fur left on the inside and a decorative flap in front. A strap wrapped around the leg held the flap in place. This boot, known as an *"endromis,"* was worn by hunters and travelers, and was sometimes used to portray the footwear of the gods. The *endromis* is sometimes pictured on Greek vases.

Buskins, similar to those worn by the Assyrians, were also worn by warriors and hunters in Greece. They were common around the fifth century B.C. and were sometimes elaborately decorated.

The Greeks wanted their gods and heroes to appear majestic in their plays. The *"kothornos,"* a shoe with a very thick sole about three inches high, was created to give tragic actors a larger-than-life appearance. The *kothornos* quickly became popular among Greek women who wanted to look taller. Soles went to great heights, and men were soon making fun of women for carrying the fashion to extremes.

Oriental fashions were popular with Greek women. They wore soft mule-style slippers at home, made of silk or some other rich fabric and embroidered with gold and pearls. Sometimes they wore sandals with their slippers to protect the delicate shoes. Women changed shoes for different occasions, having their maids bring along the necessary shoes for an outing. But such a varied shoe wardrobe was only for wealthy women concerned with fashion.

White was the predominant color for leather, but leather was also dyed scarlet, saffron, green, and black. Red soles became fashionable for some shoes. Purple was usually reserved for kings and magistrates and depictions of gods.

After Greece was conquered by Rome in 146 B.C., the Romans adopted many Greek shoe styles. The Roman version of the Greek *krepis* was called a *"crepida."* Soldiers wore the combined *cnemis* and *crepida.* And there was a Roman *"cothurnus,"* like the Greek *kothornos,* which added stature to actors, ladies, and even men of position.

Shoes were important to Romans and reflected their ideas about classes of society. Citizens, noncitizens, senators, priests, and soldiers wore footwear that was appropriate for their position in life. Anyone familiar with the set of rules for what shoes people were

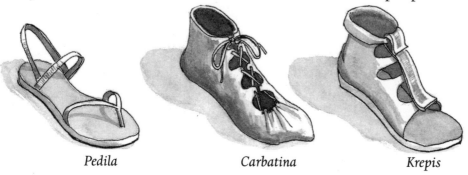

Pedila   *Carbatina*   *Krepis*

allowed to wear could tell the rank, wealth, profession, and approximate age of a Roman by the shoes he or she was wearing. People were also judged by the appearance of their shoes. Anyone who did not have his laces neatly adjusted and tied was ridiculed.

In Rome, shoemaking for the higher ranks of society was considered more of an art than a craft, and famous artists designed their shoes. There were also large shops that produced shoes in great quantities to supply the army. Other shoemakers made shoes for sale at home and in the colonies.

Roman peasants and farmers wore the "pero," a simple, well-fitted shoe or low boot of natural-colored leather, sometimes reinforced with a sole. In Rome as well as in Greece, the *carbatina* was popular for civilian footwear. The Roman version was often cut in intricate openwork patterns, forming loops to thread the tie-string. These were frequently made for children since the size could be adjusted for growing feet.

In addition to the *crepida*, Romans wore many versions of the sandal or "solea," with interesting strap arrangements and thongs. Some had thick wooden soles; some were made of woven straw much like Egyptian sandals. Those for the wealthy had gilded straps and other ornate decorations.

The main shoe worn by Roman townspeople was the "calceus," an elegant shoe that entirely encased the foot. Sometimes it was made with leather so thin that it looked more like a sock. It was fas-

Cothurnus   *Pero*   *Carbatina and Pattern*

tened with four straps that wrapped around the ankle and tied in two knots at the front. Different models were made for each level of society, distinguished by material, workmanship, color, and cost. Senators and high officials wore the black *"calceus senatorius."* A red or purple style was worn by patricians and nobility for ceremonial occasions, as well as by victorious generals returning in triumphal processions. It was known as the *"calceus patricius."* The emperor sometimes rewarded people by allowing them the privilege of wearing this shoe.

The *"caliga"* was the regulation footwear for soldiers up to the rank of centurion. This was the shoe in which the Romans conquered the world, a shoe well-designed for long marches. It looked like a sandal or open-toed boot, tied around the ankle in an intricate pattern. It was cut from a single piece of leather, sewn at the back. Sometimes the *caliga* was hobnailed; the heavy soles were studded with iron or bronze nails, for longer wear and better traction. The pattern of hobnails was designed to distribute support where it was needed, and an inner sole protected the wearer from the turned nails. These were strong, well-ventilated shoes that supported the foot and ankle well and adjusted for good fit. An army of soldiers wearing hobnailed shoes made a thunderous sound as it attacked, instilling fear in the enemy.

The emperor and the highest officials wore the *"campagus,"* an elegant, open-toed parade boot, laced at the front. Frequently, the top was decorated with a small animal's head and paws, either taken from a real animal or fashioned from gold or ivory. The emperor's *campagus* was dyed purple and ornamented with gold and jewels.

The tribes of hunter-warriors that invaded Europe were consid-

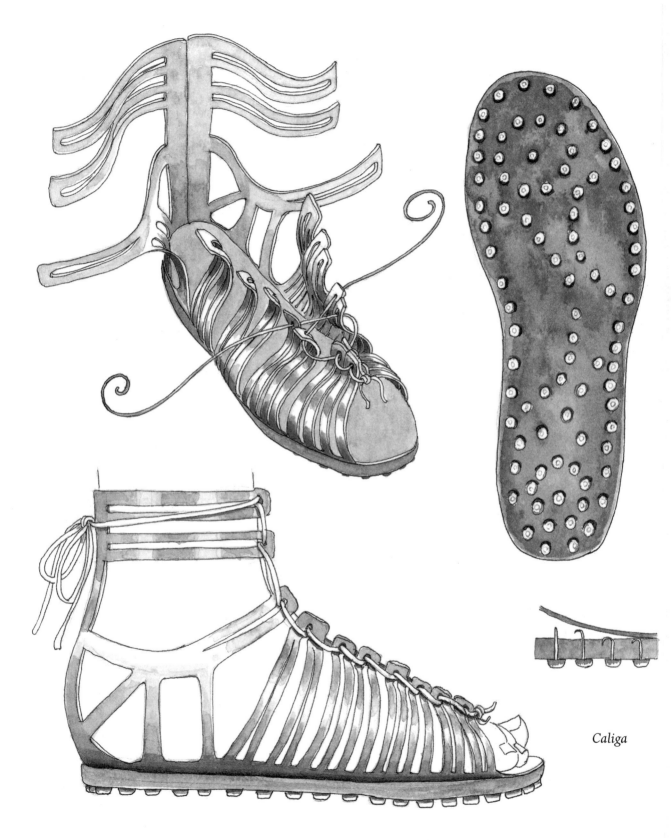

Caliga

ered uncivilized by the Romans, who called them barbarians. In colder climates these barbarians wore soft boots with the fur left on the inside. For a better fit, they tied thongs over the boots and around their legs. They also wore laced buskins, *carbatinae,* sandals, or straw slippers. Some wore low, black leather shoes with wooden soles. Long bands of leather, wool, or cloth were attached to the shoes and crisscrossed up the leg to keep hose or breeches securely fitted. Most shoes were simple, practical, and durable, but chiefs or lords often wore shoes embroidered with colored silk and yarn and had gilded bands to cross-garter their hose.

The Gauls, who settled in the southern part of France, were conquered by Rome in 58 B.C. Roman-style shoes became part of the wardrobe of both men and women of Gaul. In turn, the Gauls had a shoe that the Romans adopted, a special shoe for bad weather, made of heavy skin with a thick wooden sole. A copy of this shoe, called a *"gallica"* by the Romans, was soon being worn by Romans in the country in rainy weather. It was the ancestor of galoshes, the overshoes made of rubber or plastic still worn by some people today to protect their shoes from the rain. The spread of the Roman Empire, like the extensive trade routes of Egypt, expanded the footwear of the people.

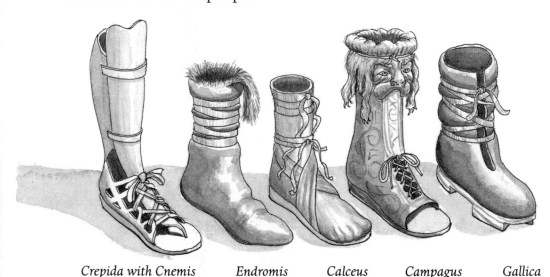

Crepida with Cnemis   *Endromis*   *Calceus*   *Campagus*   *Gallica*

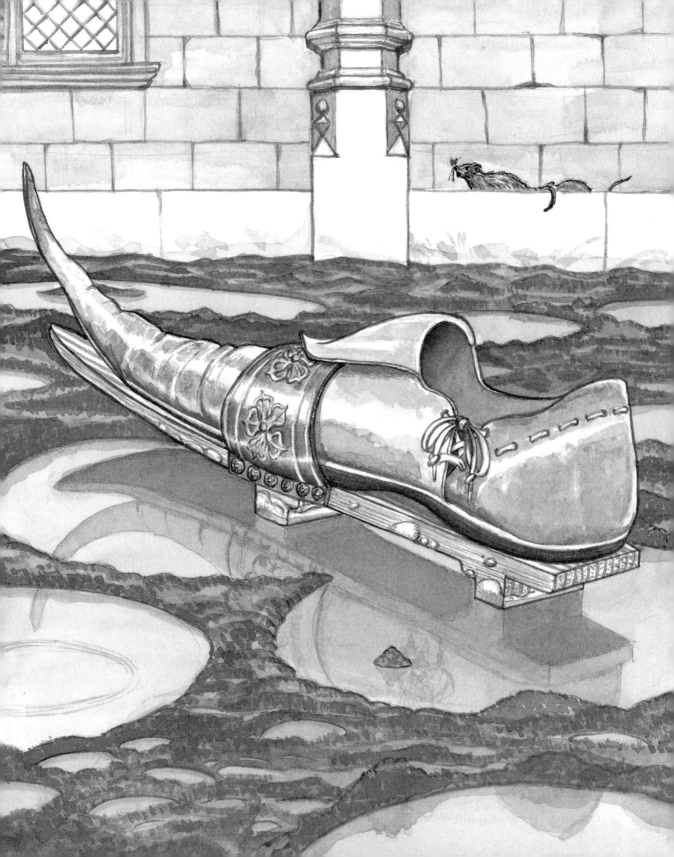

5.
Medieval Shoes

The Roman Empire split into East and West in 395 A.D. The Western Empire collapsed in 476 A.D., and Europe fell into a general state of turmoil and poverty with scattered, leaderless communities. These communities began gathering together under the leadership of separate kings and building strongholds against invaders. Inside fortified walls, people's lives became more secure, and they were able to indulge in comforts and luxuries. Most people made their own shoes or went barefoot. Skilled shoemakers, however, provided elegant footwear for wealthy nobles.

The court of the surviving Eastern Byzantine Empire influenced the fashions in the kingdoms that developed in Europe. Since the capital city of Constantinople was at the crossroads of major trade

Poulaine and Patten

routes, Byzantine shoemakers used materials and styles from Russia and Asia, such as sumptuously decorated shoes in rich velvets and satins with upturned or pointed toes.

The main footwear of the Middle Ages for both men and women in Europe was a soft-soled shoe with a foot-fitting upper and a slightly pointed toe. It could be worn on either foot. For common people it was cut simply and usually made from untanned hides. Higher-quality shoes had bands of decoration that reinforced seams or other weak places of the shoe or added support at the ankle or instep. Fine shoes were ornamented by many different techniques — stamping, embossing, painting, engraving, embroidery, or cut-out designs. People fastened their shoes in front or at the side using laces, buttons, or buckles.

People continued to wear buskins, *carbatinae,* and shoes with cross-gartering up the legs. Galoshes, also known as Gaulish shoes or *gallicae,* were still popular. Nobles wore galoshes of red leather with beautifully carved wooden soles. Many kinds of boots were in style, from short ones reaching only a few inches up the leg, to long, soft ones going to the knee. When the Christian church preached that it was sinful for feet to be exposed, sandals went out of fashion for most people.

Friars in the eleventh century began wearing sturdy, simple shoes with a broad strap across the instep, fastened with a buckle. They were frequently "straights," designed to be worn on either

Byzantine Shoe

Soft-Soled Shoe

foot. These shoes were so durable and practical that they were soon being worn by people in all walks of life. A similar style, usually called a "monk's shoe," is still worn today.

Crusaders, returning from the Holy Lands, brought back new shoe styles and new fabrics. Especially popular were silk, velvet, and gold cloth shoes with long, pointed toes and shoes with curved toes.

Craftsmen in medieval Europe were organized in associations known as guilds whose regulations kept high standards of workmanship and training. Shoemakers were originally divided into two separate guilds: "Cordwainers" were the shoe- and bootmakers. Their name came from the fine leather imported from Cordova in Spain. They made shoes of new leather and resoled and repaired shoes. "Cobblers" bought up old shoes and made them over for people who couldn't afford new shoes. They were not allowed to work with new leather. Cordwainers looked down on cobblers, and fights often broke out between them. Eventually, however, they became indistinguishable.

Our basic system of shoe sizes dates from 1324. In the reign of King Edward II of England, a measuring system was established, using three barley corns placed end to end as the standard for one inch. Shoemakers determined that thirty-nine barley corns or thirteen inches was the length of the longest foot. So thirteen became the largest shoe size, with the smaller sizes graded down from that. Although thirteen is no longer the largest size available, current sizes are still graded by one-third of an inch.

A wooden foot-shaped form, called a "last," was made in each shoe size. This served to shape either the right or left shoe. Shoemakers measured a customer's foot on a measuring stick and shaped the shoe over the appropriate last. Shoes came in two widths. Padding was placed over the last to produce the wide width.

Shoe fashions were exchanged throughout Europe. By the fourteenth century, Paris had become known for its fashionable shoes and clothing. Merchants in Venice, a major trade center, imported a French fashion doll every year to show to the Venetian ladies. This was a small mannequin made of wax, dressed in the latest Paris styles. Women used these dolls to keep up with fashion trends until they were replaced by magazines in the nineteenth century.

Brightly colored leather and fanciful decorations were popular in the fourteenth and fifteenth centuries. Wealthy people had intricate designs worked in their shoes; some were made to look like the rose windows in cathedrals. Parti-colored clothes were fashionable. A costume was divided into halves, quarters, or smaller sections that were made of contrasting colors. Right and left shoes were sometimes different colors, often matching the stocking worn on the opposite leg.

Long pointed toes on men's shoes reached fantastic lengths, often as much as twelve inches beyond the foot. Some shoes measured thirty inches from heel to toe. These "piked" shoes originally came from Cracow, Poland, and were known as *"poulaines"* in France and *"crackowes"* in England. The toes were stuffed with moss, hay, or wool or were shaped with whalebone. Many men

Monk's Shoe

Rose Window Decoration

loved the flapping sound the shoes made as they walked. Other men had the long points held up by fine chains and attached to garters at their knees. Some had tiny silver bells on the upturned toe.

Shoes of nobles were beautifully crafted of fine materials. They were so fragile and expensive that wooden soles, called "pattens," were attached to raise them above the wet and mud. Pattens often had extra thicknesses under the ball of the foot and under the heel. This made walking easier because the patten could tilt forward; it also added height without much extra weight. These were fore-runners of the high heels that would come into fashion later. The form of the patten was adapted to shoe fashions. The toes of some pattens were made long and pointed, and others curved upward to support curled-toed shoes.

Some people still wore shoes with round toes or pointed toes of reasonable length. But many styles of shoes, boots, and slippers were made with extra-long toes. Knights wore steel versions of the fashion. When they dismounted to fight on foot, they found they could not walk in their long, pointed shoes and had to break off the tips. Foot protections were later made with removable tips.

Women did not follow this fashion; the toes of their shoes were

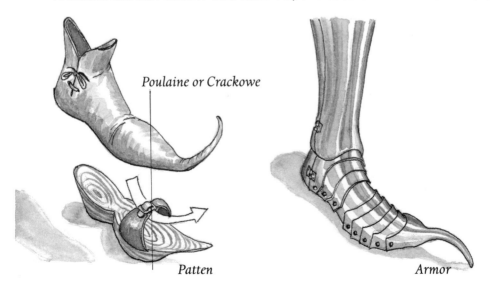

Poulaine or Crackowe

Patten

Armor

pointed, but rarely extended more than an inch or two. It was difficult enough for ladies to manipulate their long skirts and headdresses without trying to deal with outrageously long shoes.

Laws were passed to regulate the length of toes. The nobility were struggling to separate themselves from the rising middle class. They didn't like common people imitating the fashions of nobles. It was decreed that no commoner could have shoes with toes longer than six inches, and one foot was the maximum length for a gentleman. Shoes with toes longer than that were the privilege only of nobles. Rich ornamentation was also strictly limited by income. Laws and proclamations concerning fashion have been made by the church and by the government throughout the centuries. People, however, are very resistant to having their fashions regulated, and such laws are difficult to enforce.

Piked shoes were eventually outlawed in Europe. In 1463 King Edward IV of England ruled that any shoemaker who made shoes or boots with toes more than two inches long for people of low position would be fined and censured by the church. And in 1470 shoemakers in France were also prohibited from making the long-toed shoe. The up-turned toe remained popular in Eastern countries.

Round-toed slippers and mules became fashionable in Europe. Boots of all heights became popular, many with linings of a contrasting color. Some boots were almost like leather stockings, reaching to the top of the thigh. Hose with leather soles were also very popular.

Peasants wore wooden shoes, known in different parts of Europe as *"sabots," "klomps,"* or *"clogs."* Some were a mule-style shoe with a leather covering for the front of the foot nailed to a thick wooden sole. Similar clogs are still worn today. Others were made from a solid block of wood. For the people who did the ordinary work of the world, these were very practical, inexpensive shoes. Wood is a porous material that lets air circulate and absorbs sweat. Wooden shoes protect the wearer against wet and cold and are easy to clean after muddy, dirty work. In extreme cold, people found that with an insole of plaited straw, these shoes kept their feet quite warm.

Common people made their leather shoes and boots last longer by hammering nails into their soles. A crescent of iron was sometimes added to the heel.

In Scotland and Ireland a special shoe, called a "brogue," was worn. Men punched small holes in the shoe to drain out water when they waded through streams and marshlands. Later these perforations became purely decorative, often with ornamental pinked edges.

"Gillies" also came from Scotland. They were originally worn by hunting attendants and are distinguished by their unique lacing style. The laces were threaded through tube-like slots formed by turned-under edges at each side. Many of the classic shoe styles still worn today have been worn since the Middle Ages.

Wooden Shoe   Iron Crescent and Nails   Brogue   Gillie

6.
Shoes of the Renaissance

The European Renaissance, which lasted from about 1450 to 1600, was an age of renewed interest in art and science and an age of exploration and discovery. It was also a time of prosperity that led to refinement of as well as extravagance in fashion.

After having gone to ridiculous lengths, fashion went to ridiculous widths. The long-toed *poulaines* went out of fashion and a soft, broad-toed, low-cut slipper became popular. It was nicknamed the "duck's bill," "bear's paw," or "cow's mouth." This was fashionable mostly among men; women's shoes were much less extreme. Toes gradually became wider and wider, standing out as much as eight or nine inches. They were stuffed and shaped into rolls, and sometimes made to look like giant toes. Sides and backs were very low,

35

Slashed Wide-Toed Shoe

Puffed and Stuffed　　*Duck's Bill*　　*Bear's Paw*　　*Armor*

and some were completely backless. It is hard to imagine how men were able to keep them on or walk in them.

Puffed, slashed clothing with fabric of a contrasting color displayed through the slashes had become very fashionable in imitation of soldiers who used pieces of banners, tents, and whatever they could find to mend their tattered clothing. Shoes followed the fashion. Contrasting linings were pulled out through the slashes in little puffs of color. Again these styles were adapted for all types of footwear. Eventually the width of shoes was limited by law to six inches. As shoes returned to normal width and fit, slashing was still in vogue, but linings were no longer pulled through the openings and only showed as bright contrasting lines. These delicate shoes had to be protected by pattens.

The "chopine" was a variation of the patten. It was brought to Venice by traders, having originated in the Orient to raise feet above wet and muddy streets. But by the time the chopine reached European women, it had become a ridiculous, impractical fashion. Chopines were shoes on high wooden pedestals, elaborately decorated with paint, fabric, and gold, or encrusted with jewels. Sometimes they were as much as thirteen inches high. It was almost impossible to walk on these stilts, and ladies usually required assistance to move about. The chopine was one of many shoe inventions that kept women at home and inactive. Although they were hidden most of the time under long skirts, ladies loved the added height and added attention these shoes brought, and chopines became the rage among wealthy European women.

The modern heel developed from pattens and chopines. At first a cork wedge was placed between the sole and the upper to make the shoe higher at the back. Then there was a slipper with a heel, which still had a flat sole attached. Eventually the design was lightened and shaped into a shoe with a gracefully curved heel about an inch and a half to two inches high. The heel as we know it, worn solely for its appearance and the added height it offered, was first

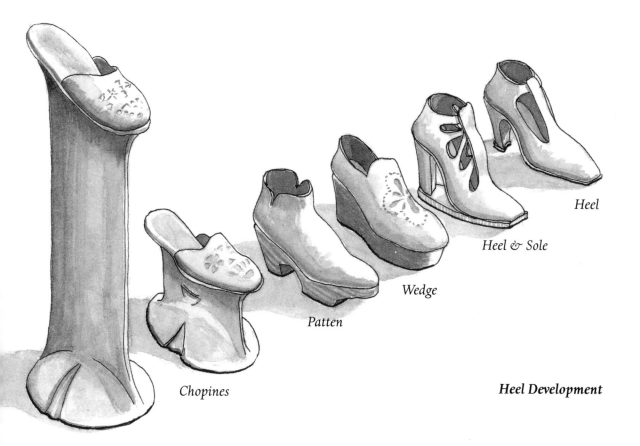

Chopines

Patten

Wedge

Heel & Sole

Heel

Heel Development

worn at Italian and Spanish courts and was popularized in France by Catherine de Medici when she became queen in 1533.

Many materials — wood, metal, and leather — were used for heels. Designers experimented with many shapes and positions for heels. And many sprained ankles and other injuries were suffered in the search for an ideal heel that gave the foot support as well as elegance. Heels were worn by both men and women. They often needed long walking sticks to help them balance on their high heels. Women not only had to master the art of walking in these new shoes, but also had to move in wide skirts shaped over a wire cage known as a farthingale. The skirt was supposed to move backward and forward as they moved, rising up a bit in front to show off the lady's beautiful heeled shoes.

The chopine and the "pantoffle" were in fashion in England at the time of Queen Elizabeth I. The pantoffle was an updated version of the mule with a cork sole. Pantoffles were often worn over fragile slippers as protection. Shoes tied with latchets were in style toward the end of the sixteenth century. The front, or "vamp," of the shoe was cut long and came up over the instep; flaps on each side of the foot were tied over the vamp. The dress and shoes of both men and women at the time of Elizabeth I were lavish displays of splendor worth fortunes, made with precious jewels and luxurious materials.

Working men and women needed boots and shoes that kept their feet dry and warm and would last a long time. They continued to wear many of the old styles. The common people were, however, aware of fashion developments. Whenever possible, they wore fashionable styles made of sturdier materials. Their wooden shoes were sometimes intricately carved and painted to imitate the slippers and heeled shoes of the wealthy.

The Renaissance was a time of exploration, and the European adventurers coming to America wore boots or low leather shoes with slashed toes. The native peoples they encountered frequently went barefoot. In South America, Mexico, and the southwestern part of the United States, some people wore grass and fiber sandals, often brilliantly colored and decorated. They usually attached their sandals with two thongs, one passing between the big toe and second toe, the other between the third and fourth toes. People of the Amazon wore rubber shoes made from the milky juice of a tropical tree. They dipped their feet, or molds of their feet, in the juice and dried them over the fire, creating custom-fitted sneakers. In the northeastern regions and on the plains, the native men and women were wearing moccasins and leggings made of softly tanned deerskin. "Moccasins" were made from a single piece of leather gathered around the foot. There might be an added flap over the top of the foot that could be worn up or down, and sometimes an additional leather sole. These shoes were often beautifully decorated with beads and porcupine quills. These would be adopted by Europeans after the Renaissance.

Pantoffle   Mayan Sandal   Moccasin

7.
Shoes of the Seventeenth Century

Europeans were settling in America during the seventeenth century. Colonists dressed as they had in Europe, saving their best clothes and shoes for special occasions and wearing sturdier attire for everyday work. Wealthy settlers depended on the ships bringing goods from Europe and imported Paris fashion dolls to keep up with the latest fashions, which did not change as rapidly as they do today. Some colonists, like the Puritans, made strict laws to control how people dressed, and those who ignored such laws were severely punished. In some cases men were imprisoned for excessive use of gold and silver laces. Other colonists had no dress restrictions. Many settlers discovered that the Indian moccasin was a comfortable shoe that could be beautifully decorated. By the end

41

of the century, they were sending these shoes to Europe. Moccasins were America's first fashion export.

The first shoemaker in America arrived in Virginia in 1619. Another came to Salem, Massachusetts, with his apprentice on the third trip of the *Mayflower* in 1629. The first tanner arrived at Lynn, Massachusetts, in 1630. Shoemakers were sometimes given special privileges to encourage them to settle in a particular town since the demand for shoes was so great in the growing country. A father sometimes apprenticed his son to a shoemaker so he could learn to make the shoes for the family. Big plantations employed full-time shoemakers. Those who could afford it bought imported shoes from Europe.

Making shoes by hand was a complicated process, using essentially the same techniques practiced by skilled artisans in ancient Rome and still employed by those making handcrafted shoes today. The shoemaker measured his customer's foot on the size stick. Wealthy customers might have custom-made lasts that were wooden models or plaster casts of their feet; but for most, the shoemaker used his standard last for the size. He cut the pieces to a general pattern. For a simple shoe style, he sewed the vamp, the part that covers the toes and top of the foot, to the counters, which covered the back and sides. This was shaped over the last. Using stretching pliers, he pulled the shoe upper tightly and tacked it to the last.

Then the shoemaker cut the sole, which had been soaking to keep it pliable. He pounded the sole with a mallet on a lapstone, a flat stone held on his lap. When it was smooth and even, he glued the sole to the upper to hold it in place for stitching. Before sewing,

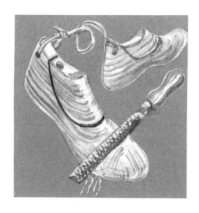 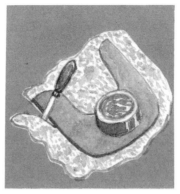 

  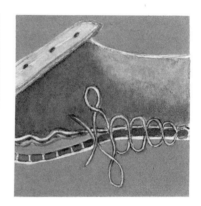

 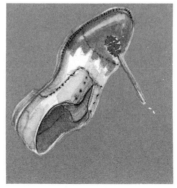 

Shoemaking

he cut a groove close to the edge of the sole. He wanted the stitches to be below the surface so they wouldn't rub against the ground when the customer walked. Next, he ran a marking wheel along the groove to mark the places to punch holes with his awl.

Then he stitched the upper and sole together, with a special double stitching. He used two hog's bristle needles with two waxed linen threads, passing both needles through the same hole, but in opposite directions.

When he had finished attaching the sole, he nailed the heel on in layers. He trimmed the sole, took out the tacks, and removed the shoe from the last. Finally, he stained and polished the shoe.

This produced a very basic-style shoe. Many designs were much more complex and required more pieces. Fine shoes usually had a lining that had to be cut, sewn, and attached.

European courts were competing with each other for new and exciting fashion ideas. Some European shoemakers became rich and famous for their beautiful workmanship. In 1663, Nicholas Lestage became a celebrity for the perfect-fitting seamless calfskin boots he made for King Louis XIV of France. He was forbidden to make another pair or reveal his secret. He had taken the skin from the leg of a calf without splitting it and shaped the skin into form in the tanning and dressing of the leather. Other shoemakers did not discover his secret until the eighteenth century.

Boots were the main footwear for men in the first part of the century. Gentlemen even wore boots indoors. At first they were high and tight-fitting. Around 1625, as longer breeches became fashionable, lower boots were worn. They were very wide at the top, and usually worn with the top folded down. Light colors like yellow, pale blue, white, and especially buff were popular. Spur leathers, large pieces of leather frequently shaped like a butterfly, were attached over the instep to conceal the spur fastenings. The boots were often worn with boot hose of sheer white linen decorated with lace and embroidery that came over the tops of the boots. Walking was very difficult with such extremely wide boots. These boots were identified with cavaliers and musketeers, so the wearer's gait became known as the "cavalier swagger." Wealthy men owned huge wardrobes of boots, some as many as three hundred pairs.

By the middle of the seventeenth century this style was replaced by a hard, shiny black boot known as the "jackboot" or "great boot." It was large enough to wear with a shoe inside, which gave it a rather clumsy look. However, being able to take off a heavy boot and have a comfortable or more elegant shoe inside made the jackboot convenient and popular. The inside top was sometimes lined with pockets for papers and small objects. The jackboot remained popular into the eighteenth century.

The "oxford" came into fashion about 1640. Oxford University students were rebelling against the boots that were in vogue and

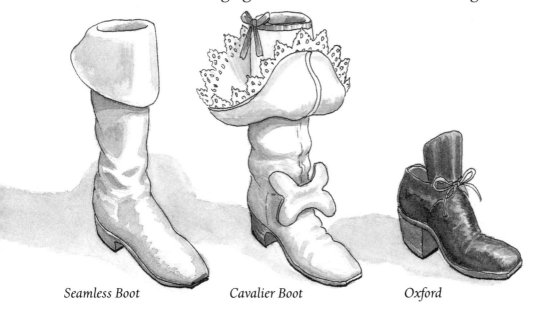

Seamless Boot   *Cavalier Boot*   *Oxford*

began wearing a cooler, more comfortable lower shoe that was laced across the instep. The oxford has gone in and out of fashion, but it is now considered a classic style.

In the last half of the century, men wore lower shoes more frequently. The vamp of the shoe was long, with square toes and high heels. Most shoes were now straights, made to be worn on either foot. It was difficult to make mirror-image lasts for shoes with heels.

Shoes differed mainly in their ornamentation. Courtiers wore gray or brown shoes with red heels and red-edged soles. Satin and brocade shoes were also popular for court wear. When the King of France had shoes with miniature scenes painted on them by a famous artist, having paintings on shoes and heels became the vogue at the French court.

Beautiful wide silk shoelaces were a popular decoration for shoes. These grew into "shoe roses," which eventually became lavish ornaments costing huge sums of money. Shoe roses were made of fine lace and silk, decorated with needlework and jewels. Sometimes an extra rosette was worn on the toe of the shoe. Some wealthy people spent as much on shoe roses as an ordinary family spent in a year. Other fashionable shoe decorations were wide stiff bows known as "butterflies" or "windmills."

Shoes with high tongues were also in fashion. Originally this was a practical idea to protect the wearer from splashes and the pebbles that kicked up from the road, without wearing a full boot. Eventually the tongues became purely decorative. They were turned back to show the contrasting lining and were sometimes scalloped or cut in a pattern. The long tongue became exaggerated, going several inches up the leg.

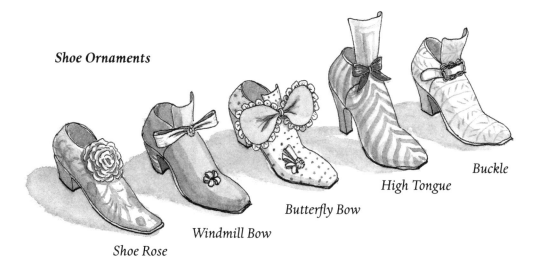

Shoe Ornaments

Shoe Rose

Windmill Bow

Butterfly Bow

High Tongue

Buckle

Toward the end of the century, shoes were fastened with a new fashion accessory, the buckle. These ornaments became a new sign of status; ordinary men wore brass or steel, the wealthy wore silver or jeweled buckles.

Heels on men's shoes were generally larger and heavier in shape than women's. Men, however, sometimes wore heels that were quite high — four and a half to five inches. Rosettes were not worn so much by women, again because their long skirts were complicated to maneuver and the costly rosettes would be hidden most of the time. Very high chopines were still worn. Small feet were fashionable, and some women bound their feet with waxed linen tape to fit them into tiny shoes. These women didn't expect to do much walking. Women wore wooden pattens, cork-soled pantoffles, or wooden-soled galoshes to protect their shoes. Pattens were sometimes made to fit and match each pair of shoes. Although it was rare for the shape of women's shoes to differ from men's, in the 1680s, pointed toes became fashionable for women's shoes, while men's shoes kept the square toe.

8.
Eighteenth Century Shoes

France set the mode for fashionable people in Europe and America during most of the eighteenth century. The reign of Louis XV was a long one, lasting from 1715 to 1774, and whatever was worn at his court was the stylish thing to wear. Men's square toes went out of fashion in the early part of the eighteenth century. They were replaced by pointed toes, a fashion that continued through the century. In fact, "old square toes" became a name used for an old-fashioned, stodgy man. By 1740, most men were wearing shoes with a low, broad heel, three-quarters to an inch in height. The colors favored for men's shoes were conservative black and brown. There was a very high standard of craftsmanship.

All decoration was focused on the buckles, which were made

Brocade Buckled Shoe

from many materials and were plain or ornamented according to the wealth and taste of the wearer. For many rich people, buckles were much more than just a fastening. They were pieces of large and ostentatious jewelry, transferred from shoe to shoe. Imaginations went wild, and fortunes were spent on them.

Boots were worn mainly by sportsmen and soldiers. The "top boot" was a popular style that fit around the leg almost like a stocking. The top was turned down to show a contrasting cuff. Often the boot was of blackened, grained leather and the cuff showed the flesh side of the leather, which had been left brown. Fancier versions had linings of lighter, softer leather at the cuffs. The very finest were made without seams, using the method that had once been the secret of Lestage. For those who could not afford this luxury, a seamless look was imitated by concealing the back seam with a special paste.

The Hessian mercenaries hired by George III to fight the rebellious American colonists wore shiny, black leather boots with gold or silver braid at the top and a silk tassel dangling from the front peaked top. These "hessians" were scoffed at in comparison with

Low Broad-Heeled Shoe   *Top Boot*   *Hessian*

the elegant top boot, but had become the height of fashion by the end of the century.

Women wore shoes with pointed toes and slim, gracefully curved heels, which were made of wood and painted or covered with leather or fabric. Sometimes rhymes were written on the heel, or jewels were set in a pattern. The slippers were made of silk, satin, brocade, wool, and linen, lined with kid and often enhanced with a beautiful buckle.

Pattens and clogs were still a necessity for walking outdoors. Pattens were carefully made to match shoes, their straps sometimes of the same material as the shoe. Iron rings might be attached to the sole to raise the pattens off the ground. Frequently the sole was hinged to make walking easier. Clogs were designed to protect heels and prevent them from digging into soft ground. Some shoes with heels had a flat sole, called a "slap sole," attached. People also wore flat-soled overshoes with only a toe cap. All styles of overshoes were noisy and had to be removed in church and other quiet places.

Both men and women wore indoor slippers, which served the same purpose as bedroom slippers do today. They were comfortable mule-style slippers in a variety of materials and colors.

Although the French government was nearly bankrupt by the time Louis XVI and his queen, Marie Antoinette, came to the throne in 1774, they maintained an extravagant lifestyle. The shoes of the French court had become walking jewel boxes. Marie Antoinette had so many shoes to match her wardrobe, she needed an index to keep track of them. These excesses in fashion were very unpopular with the people.

When the French Revolution brought an end to the monarchy in

1791, shoe styles changed dramatically. Wearing anything associated with the aristocracy was not merely politically incorrect; it was dangerous. Red heels disappeared; cord and ribbon ties replaced buckles. Buckles, so popular in the French court, became symbols of everything that was hated about the nobility. Americans, having already demonstrated their independent nature, wore buckles somewhat longer than Europeans. Still the buckle industry, which had employed thousands of workers and at one time turned out 2,500,000 buckles a year, was doomed.

People thought of Greece and Rome as a high point of civilized culture, and fashion looked to their styles for inspiration. Contemporary adaptations of the sandal, buskin, and *cothurnus* became fashionable. Some women shocked society by appearing in sandals without stockings, and wearing jeweled toe rings. The flat, heelless slipper, or *"escarpin,"* with a small ribbon bow, was widely worn and even made at home.

In America, men still wore cowhide shoes with large buckles. Heels were generally lower and ornaments less outrageous. The wealthy were aware of the French fashions, but fashions were never so extreme in America. Some American shoemakers were creating their own designs, not just copying European fashions. Shoes did not set people apart so much in America as in Europe.

Escarpin

Mule

Slap Sole

Patten with Iron Ring

Shoe and Patten Set

American Buckled Shoe

Lynn, Massachusetts, became the center of the thriving shoe-making industry in America. In 1750 John Dagyr opened a workshop where each worker was trained to do one operation in the making of the shoe. During slow periods, when there were not many orders, shoes were produced for general sale. At first people couldn't believe that anything as personal as a shoe could be made this way; however, the convenience of buying shoes without waiting began to appeal to customers. Some shoemakers began selling ready-made shoes in general stores or from horse-drawn carts that traveled from place to place. In 1793 the first retail shop opened in Boston, where people could purchase ready-made shoes on Wednesdays and Saturdays.

The middle class in Europe wore sturdy leather shoes, wooden shoes, sandals, buskins, and durable brogues. Some peasants still wore cross-gartering. But the revolutions in America and France, and the growing spirit of equality, were beginning to narrow the gap between the wealthy and the common people, and this applied to footwear as well.

9.
Nineteenth Century Shoes

The French Revolution had far-reaching effects, even in fashions. Many designers fled to England, and London became an important fashion center. Although Paris regained its important position in creating women's styles, London became established as the trendsetter for men.

Important military events were taking place in Europe in the early part of the nineteenth century; and during the Napoleonic Wars, shoes reflected a military spirit. England was famous for its high-quality boots, and boots with spurs were worn by men of all classes in both civilian and military life. There were many styles and heights, named for the different leaders associated with them. Hessians and top boots were still worn. Wellingtons were sup-

High Buttoned Boot

posed to have been designed by the great British general, although he is usually shown wearing hessians. The "wellington" was a close-fitting, shiny black boot cut straight across the top with a simple binding.

Blücher, Wellington's German ally at the battle of Waterloo in 1815, was credited with designing the "blucher boot" in which the quarters (or side pieces) lapped over the vamp and laced over the instep. The idea was not really new for low shoes but it was a new style for boots.

Some men wore their boots in the drawing room and for dancing. For most formal occasions, men wore low-heeled black pumps, usually laced with one or two pairs of lacing holes. Square, pointed, and oval toes were all acceptable styles. Leather finished to a hard glossy shine by a special patented process was the new material. Everyone wanted high-gloss shoes, and patent-leather fulfilled this desire.

Women wore pumps similar to those of men. Another popular style for women was a dainty, low, flat shoe with a ribbon that crossed and tied at the ankles. Dancing was very popular in the nineteenth century. Women's dance shoes were very delicate, and

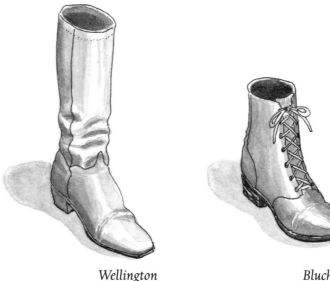

Wellington   *Blucher*

Men's Evening Pumps   *Women's Shoes with Crisscrossed Ribbons*

it was not unusual for a lady to wear out a pair of shoes before the evening was over.

Josephine, the Empress of France and wife of Napoleon I, was a fashion idol to women at the beginning of the century. She spent a fortune on clothes and had, at one count, 521 pairs of shoes. The count changed hourly, since she changed her clothes four or five times a day and sometimes tossed her shoes away after wearing them. Some of her slippers were so delicately made that they were intended only to be admired when she was seated, never to be walked in.

When Victoria was crowned Queen of England in 1837, beginning the Victorian era of fashion that would last throughout the century, boots became the predominant fashion in footwear for men, women, and children. They were in style even for dress occasions. The queen's bootmaker presented her with his own invention — boots with elastic inserts at the sides. They could stretch to go on easily and return to their original, trimly fitted shape. And there was no need for fasteners. Shoes with elastic gores were immediately popular with men as well. The idea spread to America, where they were known as "congress boots."

Buttoned boots were also popular, even though they required special buttonhooks to fasten and unfasten them. They were made of leather, fabric, or a combination of contrasting materials. Reptile, alligator, and kangaroo skins were new materials used for contrasts, as well as patent-leather and sueded leather, with the flesh side given a velvety finish. These boots usually fastened on the outside ankle. Some had as many as fourteen buttons, and some were made with scalloped buttonhole edges. Fashionable women and young girls forced their feet into the smallest possible boots. Often the boots were so tight that their legs bulged above them.

Men's boots and shoes had square toes that often turned up. They were not made that way, but having up-turned toes was a fad among young men, who produced the desired effect by sitting with their toes against the wall. Women's boots and shoes had square toes, but they were usually much narrower.

In the 1850s, the "balmoral shoe," or "bal," was made fashionable for men by Prince Albert. It was a high shoe closed with laces. It had five or six eyelets that gave the shoe a very trim, well-fitted look. The royal family had built Balmoral Castle in Scotland as a country home and everything new and smart was called "balmoral."

Gore Boot   *Buttoned Boot*   *Balmoral*

"Bottines" became the stylish shoes for ladies and girls. Made of fabric that matched the women's dresses, they rose several inches above the ankle and laced at the back, front, or side. Leather toe-caps were sometimes added. Fur-lined versions were worn in cold weather.

In the 1850s Empress Eugenie of France persuaded an English designer, Charles Frederick Worth, to come to Paris. He established a fashion house that designed clothes for European royalty and for wealthy, fashion-conscious women. He was the first to show his creations on live models. Stylish boots in Paris had very high heels, very thin soles, and were either buttoned at the side or laced up the front. Patent-leather hessians were also popular for women.

In America shoemaking was being revolutionized by machines and was changing from a handcraft to a manufacturing business. Shoes were made in great quantities during the Civil War. The army was supplied with shoes made for right and left feet. The soldiers liked them and wanted them when they returned from war. Most shoes had been straights since the introduction of heels, and many thought of this new innovation as "crooked shoes." There was much debate over whether or not they were an improvement. People with flat feet, corns, gout, or rheumatism found them uncomfortable. And many people had learned that alternating their shoes every day made them last longer. Women were slower to adopt the new shoes than men, but eventually rights and lefts became preferred by most people and have stayed popular.

Fashions changed toward the end of the century. Boots remained in vogue, but there was a trend toward more comfortable footwear. Men began wearing ankle boots for winter and oxfords for summer. Oxfords were sometimes worn in the winter as well, with short "gaiters" or "spats." These were cloth or leather leg coverings that went over the instep and up to the ankle or knee. Gentlemen wore them to protect their trousers from being splashed and soiled. They gave the appearance of boots with contrasting tops.

For evening and dress occasions, men wore black patent-leather pumps with a black grosgrain bow. The d'Orsay pump was cut into a low "V" on the sides. Mules were the lounging slippers for both men and women. High heels became popular again with women for shoes, boots, and slippers. Evening slippers for ladies were ornamented with large bows and buckles.

Many women, however, were entering professions and taking up sports. They needed more practical, sensible shoes. Oxfords and sturdy, laced boots with a medium heel were the choice of more active women. Tennis, boating, and bicycling became very fashionable in the nineties, and canvas shoes with rubber soles were the new sports shoe.

Rubber had been known for a long time, but it became sticky in

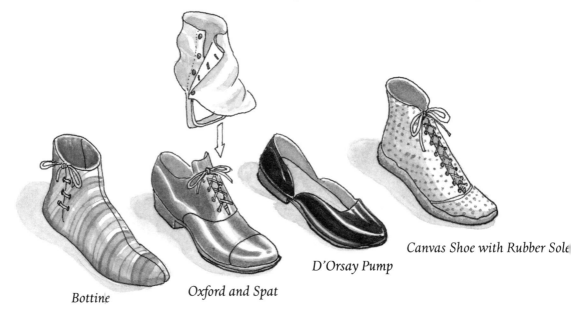

Bottine

Oxford and Spat

D'Orsay Pump

Canvas Shoe with Rubber Sole

summer and brittle in winter. Vulcanization, a new process, patented in 1839, made it a practical material. In addition to rubber soles, there were rubber heels, rubber galoshes, and rubber wellingtons.

By the end of the century, shoes were being made mostly by machines. Ready-to-wear shoes were replacing shoes made to order. Magazines were telling women which shoes were appropriate for day wear, evenings, and different activities and occasions. A wide range of shoe styles in a variety of materials was becoming available to more people than ever before.

10.
Twentieth Century Shoes

Wars often inspire shoe styles and influence increases in production. With the need to supply shoes for soldiers in the Civil War, the United States had developed most of the technology for the manufacture of shoes and took the lead in producing low-priced shoes in an interesting variety of styles. Again, during the First World War, factories expanded to make shoes in quantity for the soldiers. After the war, handmade shoes became extremely rare. With increased production, shoe styles and fashions have been changing and overlapping rapidly throughout the century.

The role of shoemakers changed. Previously they had been skilled artisans who produced the goods ordered by their customers. Now they were becoming the designers. As they became

Alligator Spike-Heeled Court Shoe

famous for their work, it was prestigious to own shoes made by certain designers.

In the first decade of the century, men still wore front-laced boots or high shoes in winter and oxfords or low button shoes for summer. High, buttoned, or laced shoes with contrasting tops and toes were still in vogue for women in the early part of the century. Women also wore suede or patent-leather boots with the new fastener, the zipper.

In 1915, white sport shoes strapped with black or brown leather, known as "saddle shoes," first became fashionable. The Prince of Wales popularized many sports styles in the 1920s. He wore gillies with their distinct lacing and crepe-soled shoes which had the heel and sole made in one piece.

Oxfords and brogues were fashionable everyday shoes for men and women, sometimes with the "kiltie tongue," a long tongue that folded over, covering the lacing. It was often fringed for a decorative effect. For evening, men still wore black patent-leather pumps with a ribbon bow, but patent-leather oxfords were also becoming popular.

As women's hemlines went up, shoes became more important and more interesting. Heeled pumps, known as "court shoes," became classic women's footwear. They were worn as everyday shoes and dress shoes. The heels, toes, cut of the vamp, as well as the colors, materials, and ornamentation were changed in endless variations.

The thirties and forties were dominated by the Great Depression, the threat of war, and the Second World War, with Hollywood offering escape from all these problems. There were many wartime shortages. People bought shoes that were durable.

Women were employed in jobs that had once been held by men and wore pants with serviceable shoes that had heavier soles and heavy medium-sized heels. Wedge soles, platforms, and shoes with a bulkier look had originally become fashionable in Paris in the mid-thirties as a revival of Italian Renaissance styles. Lightweight cork was used for the soles, and the uppers could be made in a variety of materials. They became popular wartime shoes because they did not require leather, which was in short supply.

With the wartime shortages, designers experimented with new shoe materials. They worked with plastics, imitation leathers, raffia, cork, and many unusual animal skins, such as antelope, pigskin, ostrich, dolphin, sharkskin, and fishskin. Shoes became more colorful, since shoemakers found it was good for morale and hid imperfections in the materials. Unusual materials inspired the artistic talents of some designers.

After the Second World War, there was a move toward more delicate shoes. Wartime experimentation had led to many innovations and improvements in shoes, as well as many strange and exotic shoes. Lighter, more durable materials were developed. Shoes were often creations of fantasy. Designers made "invisible" shoes with transparent plastics, and high cantilevered shoes that were supported only at the toe and had no heel.

Men's shoe styles were changing less frequently. They wore oxfords, brogues, loafers, and monk's shoes. Oxford-style shoes replaced the classic pump for evening. After centuries of ornate footwear, most twentieth-century men were wearing only three or four styles of shoes, and all of them looked similar from a distance.

Women's shoes became more variable. Ankle straps, open toes, and the new sling backs, with a strap at the back of the heel, were

Saddle Shoe   Kiltie Tongue   Court   Sling Back   Ankle Strap

fashionable. Classic styles were updated with new colors and variations, and with wedges or platforms. The stiletto or spike heel became a very popular fashion, though it was one that damaged both floors and feet. With the stiletto, as with other crazes, there was little that foot experts could do in a battle against fashion.

Sun bathing was popular, and both men and women began wearing sandals again, as well as resort shoes. The *"huarache,"* an ancient Mexican sandal, became fashionable.

In the fifties and sixties teenagers became the fashion leaders. Movies and television spread new styles quickly around the world and there was a constant effort to come up with new ideas. People had more freedom to choose; there were no longer set fashion rules for all.

Boots were available in all fabrics, heights, styles, colors, with all kinds of soles, heels, and fastenings. Women wore vinyl boots, stretch boots, laced "granny" boots, cowboy boots, and cut-out boots. Men wore cowboy boots, combat boots, and boots made popular by the Beatles with narrow pointed toes, heels about two and a half inches high, elastic side panels, and loops for pulling them on.

Wedge   Platform   Cantilevered   Open-Toed   Huarache

Oxford Brogue Loafer Monk's Shoe Running Shoe

Shoes identified people with particular groups or beliefs. Alienation and rebellion were shown by wearing outrageous shoes — steel-capped or zippered shoes — or just by writing slogans on a pair of shoes.

Later, as health-consciousness became important, many comfortable shoe designs were mixed with all styles of clothing. Running shoes and walking shoes have become a widespread fashion, worn in all parts of the world, by people of all ages, and turning up at all occasions.

The length of time we wear a pair of shoes has been getting shorter. Often we buy new shoes more because the fashion has changed than because our old ones have worn out or because our size has changed. Many shoes are not made to wear well because they are not intended to stay in fashion for long. Shoe designers look to every period for inspiration and recombine basic shoe ideas, changing scale, proportion, color, and materials to create new fashion looks.

Vinyl Boot Granny Boot Stretch Boot Combat Boot Beatle Boot

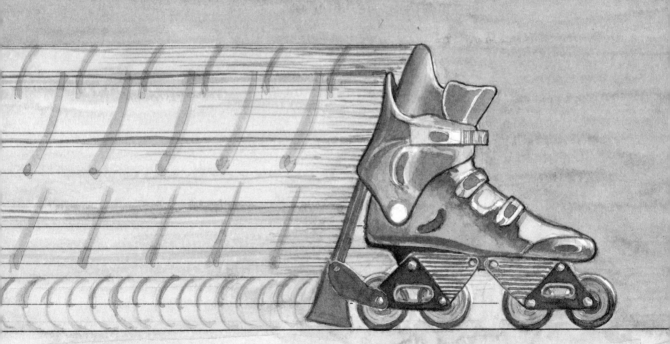

11.
Special Shoes

Many shoes have been designed to solve specific problems. Charles I, King of England from 1625 to 1649, suffered from rickets when he was a child. A bootmaker designed boots for him with brass supports in them.

Special shoes are required for certain kinds of work. Steel-capped shoes were invented in 1925 to protect workers from heavy objects falling on their toes. Some workers need shoes that have been treated to resist water, chemicals, oil, or abrasions. People whose work includes a lot of standing and walking need cushioning to relieve foot stress. Workers in mines or meatpacking plants need insulation against the cold. Special treads have been designed for people working on slippery surfaces. Sewage workers and fishermen protect themselves with body boots.

Firefighters' boots have to solve a complex set of problems. They need to be fireproof and waterproof and to protect the firefighter from rubble, debris, and broken glass. They must grip well on slippery surfaces and on the rungs of ladders. In addition, they need pads for kneeling and crawling, they must be easy to put on quickly, and they should be visible in smoky conditions.

In the mid-nineteenth century, when the American West was being settled, cowboys developed a special boot for their work. High heels kept their feet from slipping out of the stirrups and helped them brace their feet when roping an animal. The pointed toes slipped into the stirrup easily. Soles were thin enough to give the cowboy a feel for the stirrup, and the wide tops allowed air to circulate. Some cowboys added stitching to keep the boot from wrinkling, and soon many boots had elaborate decorations.

Cowboy Boot

Many dancers need special shoes. Ballerinas danced in shoes with slender, gracefully curved high heels until the 1800s, when the ribbon-tied satin shoes were developed. Now a ballerina supports herself on a single big toe and her shoes have pads of foam, wool, fur, or plastic. Tap dancers wear latchet ties or oxfords that have metal plates attached to the toes and heels of the sole. Some of the taps are plain and some have buttons that jingle.

Scandinavians and Mongolians in Asia glided over ice and snow in long, wooden shoes called "skis," narrow boat-like sliders about three to eight feet long with turned-up points. People of the Arctic also wore "snowshoes" for traveling over snow and ice. The frame was made by steaming and shaping wood and was strung with a netting of sinew or rawhide strips.

Ice skating has been a pastime in the far northern countries for centuries. Early skates had bone slides lashed on with strips of cloth. Later blades were made of wood, and eventually, iron. Ice skating was known in England in the Middle Ages, but it became popular in the middle of the sixteenth century. Skates with metal runners were brought to America by European settlers.

Roller skates were invented in Holland so that people could continue to enjoy skating in the summer. At first, the skates were made with wooden spools that were attached to shoes with leather straps, but the wood cracked easily. Later, metal casters with ball bearings were used. Until recently very few people had special shoes for roller skating. The wheels were on a metal frame that was attached to their shoes with clamps and ankle straps.

Sports that became popular in the second half of the nineteenth century required new styles of footwear. Laced, fabric shoes with

Sports Shoe

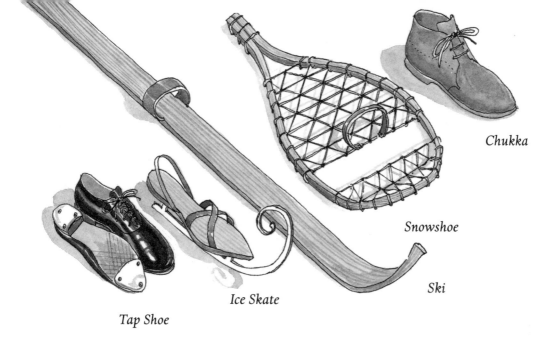

Chukka

Snowshoe

Ski

Ice Skate

Tap Shoe

rubber soles were adopted for tennis, croquet, running, and other sports. Some sports shoes were high, laced leather boots with nails on the soles to prevent slipping. Boots were worn for horseback riding, and "chukkas," the ankle-high laced boots of polo players, became popular for walking.

The 1970s saw an increased emphasis on fitness. People were taking part in physical activities in larger numbers than ever before. Interest in better sports shoes increased. Designers and inventors have been studying the movements and forces involved in walking, running, and other activities to develop better shoes with more cushioning and support. Shoe companies have hired scientists to help improve their shoes. New stronger, lighter materials have been developed for the uppers and new shock-absorbing materials are being used in the soles. Now there are special shoes for every activity.

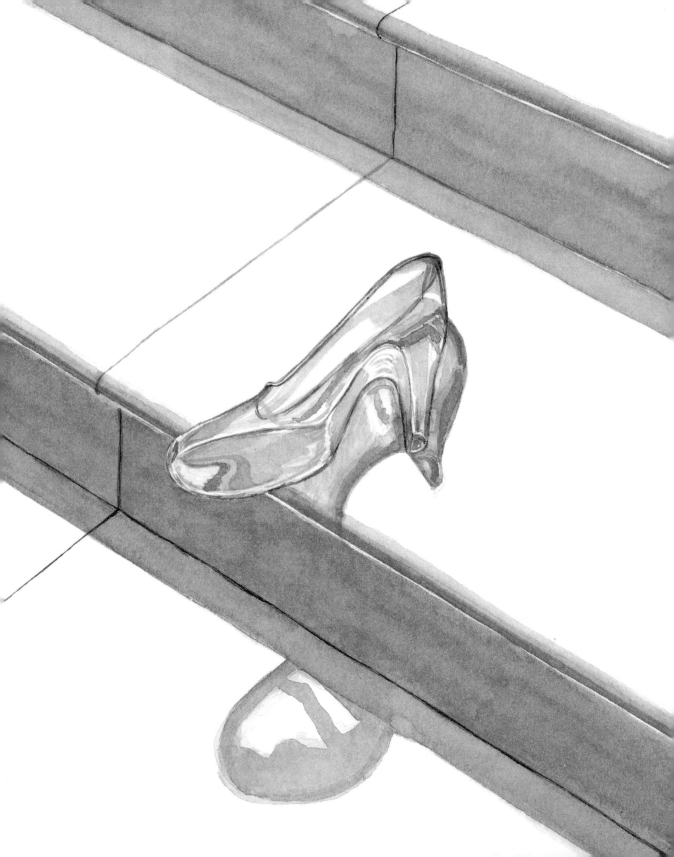

12.
Magic Shoes

It is not surprising that there are many shoe customs and superstitions, or that shoes play important roles in stories around the world. Shoes are our contact point with the earth.

Shoe customs had already developed in ancient Egypt, where some practices were similar to those of many other early peoples. An Egyptian removed his shoes in the presence of a superior to imply that he considered himself that person's servant. Shoes were not worn in sacred places because they had walked in worldly places, and the worshiper wished to cast aside all that was unholy. Many early priests wore only papyrus or plant-fiber sandals because they didn't want to contaminate themselves by wearing a dead animal. Present-day Moslems take off their shoes to pray.

In Japan people still remove their shoes when entering a house. In ancient times, Egyptians, Greeks, and Romans removed their shoes before eating. Sometimes a host would bathe the feet of his guests. In Mongolia people still believe that taking off shoes before eating helps digestion.

Throwing shoes for luck has long been a tradition in many places. An Anglo-Saxon bride threw a shoe to her wedding attendants as brides today throw bouquets. The one who caught the shoe would be the first to marry. Shoes thrown after departing ships were believed to carry good fortune with them. Today shoes are sometimes attached to the back of the newlyweds' car to bring good luck.

In Mexico a man wore red shoes if he wanted to show that he was looking for a wife. A woman in Sicily who wanted a husband would sleep with a shoe under her pillow. Some Greek women burned the shoe of a lost lover to get him back. In some Arab countries, a man could divorce his wife by putting her shoes outside his

door. In other cultures a shoe outside the door only signified that the person wanted to be left alone and undisturbed.

In the Middle Ages special celebrations were held on October 25, the feast day of Saint Crispin and Saint Crispianus, the patron saints of shoemakers. Sometimes cobbler's tools are called "Saint Hugh's bones" from a legend that, after his martyrdom, the saint's friends made tools from his bones.

Children in Holland set their wooden shoes by the fireplace on the eve of Saint Nicholas's birthday, December 6, placing a carrot or some hay in the shoe for St. Nicholas's white horse. The next morning they found toys and candy in their shoes.

Shoes have played a leading role in fairy tales and other literature. A story similar to *Cinderella* was known in ancient Egypt, where a tiny shoe convinced the Pharaoh that he must seek and marry its owner. In some versions of *Cinderella,* the stepsisters have gone as far as to cut off toes to try to fit into the little slipper.

Shoes have also been used as a symbol of ownership. Men would claim land by placing a foot on it or giving a shoe to symbolize the transfer of property. Modern children sometimes leave a shoe to hold their place in a line or in a game. In an ancient Indian epic, when King Rama was forced into exile, he left a pair of his shoes as his representative. If unjust decisions were made, his shoes jumped and made a lot of noise in protest.

In *Puss-in-Boots,* a cat wearing footwear accomplished great things. A kind and industrious shoemaker received help from elves in *The Elves and the Shoemaker.* Leprechauns could sometimes be found by listening for the tapping sound they made working on shoes. Men risked their lives to find out how the princesses wore out their shoes in *The Twelve Dancing Princesses.* Dorothy traveled through Oz in her magic slippers. There have been stories of winged shoes, of seven-league boots, and red shoes that would not let the wearer stop dancing.

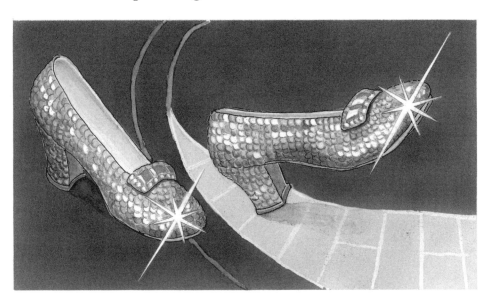

People have many superstitions about the ways in which shoes can affect their fortune:

- A pair of shoes left too far apart will bring bad luck.
- Avoid entering a house left shoe first.
- Never put shoes on a shelf above your head.
- Don't walk with one shoe off.
- Cutting fingernails on a Thursday might bring new shoes.
- If your shoelace is untied, someone is thinking of you.
- Putting your right foot in your left shoe is unlucky.
- Lying with a heavy boot on your stomach will cure a stomach ache.
- To avoid nightmares, place a pair of shoes, heels outward, at the head of the bed.

13.
Shoe Detectives

What do our feet and the coverings we put on them really say about us? Footprints are as unique as fingerprints. Most people have one foot that is larger than the other, usually the right foot, and a dominant foot, the foot one uses to kick a ball. It is usually, but not always, the same as the dominant hand.

Each person has an individual way of standing and walking. The length of step varies, as well as the distance between feet. Some people walk with their feet turned out, and some with them turned in. Some people walk briskly; some amble. A person's ankles may roll inward or out toward the sides of the feet.

Some people's legs do not form straight lines when they are standing. They may be "knock-kneed." That means that the feet are apart and the knees are touching. If there is a space between the knees when the feet are together, the person is called "bow-legged." The arches of some feet are higher or lower than normal. Some people have flat feet. Their feet flatten out completely when they are standing.

Shoes can provide clues to how an individual stands and walks. If the soles and heels are wearing down evenly, the owner probably has well-formed, well-balanced feet. Someone whose soles are worn down more on the outside, or on the inside, or in one partic-ular spot on the heel, probably has foot problems. Foot problems are also indicated if the uppers are bent and twisted out of shape, or if they have lumpy bulges, or tend to get scuffed in one spot.

Shoeprints are often found at the scene of a crime. Casts and photographs of prints are made as soon as possible, since they are easily destroyed. Forensic laboratories are frequently asked to com-pare a suspect's shoes with shoeprints. They also compare frag-ments imbedded in the shoe with specimens from the crime scene. Sometimes shoeprints reveal something that will help identify a suspect. Prints can help establish the number of people involved in a crime, the way they entered and left the premises, and their size and build. Even partial footmarks can be important.

Many men wear the same pair of shoes most of the time. If a man commits a series of crimes, he will often be wearing the same shoes. By comparing shoeprints, methods of entry, use of tools, and other evidence, detectives can link a suspect to several crimes.

Many sole patterns, especially those on athletic shoes, are dis-tinctive. Some have wavy or zigzag lines. Others have concentric circles, letters, or numerals as part of their pattern. Forensic scientists keep coded collections of the common sole patterns. Sometimes they can determine the exact brand and style of shoe from a shoeprint or identify a full sole pattern from partial marks.

Cracks and cuts on the sole of the shoe that are a normal part of everyday wear can provide evidence. In one case, a woman sued her landlord for injuries from a fall. She claimed he had not adequately cleared away ice. The insurance investigators noticed that the sole of her shoe was cracked. She claimed this was a result of her fall. Her landlord claimed the fall was caused by wearing broken shoes. Experts examining the crack and stains on the shoe lining determined that she had been wearing the cracked shoes for some time before her fall. The woman settled out of court for far less than her original demand of one hundred thousand dollars in damages.

No two feet are exactly alike or function in the same way, so it is often possible to tell whether two pieces of footwear were worn by the same person. Sometimes identifying footprints can be taken from the inside sole of a shoe. Wear patterns of the shoes and the linings are the most significant pieces of information in comparing shoes.

Since feet must provide a base to support the body, forensic scientists have worked out ratios between foot length and height and maximum foot width and weight. These vary slightly for men, women, and children, and for right and left feet; but scientists can estimate height and build from footprints. This is also used with prehistoric footprints found in caves to make guesses about the size of the people who left them. For a very rough estimation, footprint length can be figured as approximately fifteen percent of a person's height. If there are enough prints, forensic tracking specialists can often give a very good description of a subject. Besides height and weight, they can sometimes make guesses about the person's sex, age, and whether he or she is right-handed or left-handed. They might determine if the person suffered any injuries, and even if he had been carrying something.

Shoes reveal many things about the physical appearance, the personality, and the character of the wearer. Shoes can be artistic; they can be witty. Like all good design, shoes can enhance the quality of life. They can lift a person's spirits or give confidence to the insecure. Sometimes practical and sometimes foolish, our shoes always have things to tell about the human beings who design and wear them.

Bibliography

Asterisk (*) indicates books of interest to younger readers.

Alexander, R. McNeill. *Exploring Biomechanics: Animals in Motion.* New York: Scientific American Library, 1992.

*Badt, Karin Luisa. *On Your Feet!* Chicago: Children's Press, 1994.

Beard, Tyler. *The Cowboy Boot Book.* Layton, Utah: Gibbs Smith, Peregrine Smith, 1992.

Birkett, John. "Scientific Scene Linking." *Journal of the Forensic Science Society* 29, 4 (July/August 1989): 271–84.

Bodziak, William J. "Manufacturing Processes for Athletic Shoe Outsoles and Their Significance in the Examination of Footwear Impression Evidence." *Journal of Forensic Sciences* 31, 1 (January 1986): 153–76.

Boyer, G. Bruce. "Stepping Out: Custom-Made Shoes Pamper Your Feet in Style." *Cigar Aficionado,* Winter 1994.

Brooke, Iris. *Footwear: A Short History of European and American Shoes.* New York: Theatre Arts Books, 1971.

Cavanagh, Peter R. *The Running Shoe Book.* Mountain View, Calif.: Anderson World, 1980.

*Connolly, Peter. *Pompeii.* Oxford, England: Oxford University Press, 1990.

Cowie, Denise. "If the Shoe Fits . . . So, Who'd Wear It?" *Philadelphia Inquirer,* 9 October 1994, E1, 6.

Cressman, L. S. *The Sandal and the Cave: The Indians of Oregon.* Portland, Ore.: Champoeg Press/Beaver Books, 1962.

Davis, R. J., and DeHaan, J. D. "A Survey of Men's Footwear." *Journal of the Forensic Science Society* 17 (1977): 271–85.

Facy, O. E., Hannah, I. D., and Rosen, D. "Shoe Wear Patterns and Pressure Distribution Under Feet and Shoes, Determined by Image Analysis." *Journal of the Forensic Science Society* 32, 1 (1992): 15–25.

Fairservis, Walter A. *Costumes of the East.* Riverside, Conn.: Chatham Press, 1971.

Fawcett, A. S. "The Role of the Footmark Examiner." *Journal of the Forensic Science Society* 10, 1 (January 1970): 227–44.

*Fisher, Leonard Everett. *The Shoemakers.* Colonial American Craftsmen series. New York: Franklin Watts, 1967.

Footwear Industries of America. *Shoepedia: An Encyclopedia of Shoe Facts.* Reprint of 1946 ed. Davenport, Iowa: Amazon Drygoods.

Fowler, Brenda. "Forgotten Riches of King Tut: His Wardrobe." *New York Times,* 25 July 1995, C1, 10.

Fox, Richard H., and Cunningham, Carl L. *Crime Scene Search and Physical Evidence Handbook.* Washington, D.C.: U.S. Department of Justice, Law Enforcement Assistance Administration, 1985.

Garrett, Valery M. *Traditional Chinese Clothing in Hong Kong and South China, 1840–1980.* Images of Asia series. Oxford, England: Oxford University Press, 1987.

Giles, Eugene, and Vallandigham, Paul H. "Height Estimation from Foot and Shoeprint Length." *Journal of Forensic Sciences* 36, 4 (July 1991): 1134–51.

Goldfinger, Eliot. *Human Anatomy for Artists.* Oxford, England: Oxford University Press, 1991.

Gordon, Claire C., and Buikstra, Jane E. "Linear Models for the Prediction of Stature from Foot and Boot Dimensions." *Journal of Forensic Sciences* 37, 3 (May 1992): 771–82.

Groom, P. S., Lawton M. E., and Cooper, A. "Are They a Pair?" *Journal of the Forensic Science Society* 27, 3 (May/June 1987): 189–92.

Hope, Thomas. *Costumes of the Greeks and Romans.* New York: Dover, 1962.

Houston, Mary G. *Ancient Egyptian, Mesopotamian and Persian Costume & Decoration. A Technical History of Costume,* vol. I, 2nd ed. London: Adam & Charles Black, 1954.

———. *Ancient Greek, Roman and Byzantine Costume & Decoration. A Technical History of Costume,* vol. II, 2nd ed. London: Adam & Charles Black, 1959.

———. *Medieval Costume in England and France. A Technical History of Costume,* vol. III. London: Adam & Charles Black, 1939.

"If the Shoe Fits." *American Bar Association Journal* (July 1985): 34.

James, Peter, and Thorpe, Nick. *Ancient Inventions.* New York: Ballantine, 1994.

*James, Simon. *Ancient Rome.* New York: Knopf, 1990.

Jay, C. B., and Grubb, M. J. "Defects in Polyurethane-Soled Athletic Shoes — Their Importance to the Shoeprint Examiner." *Journal of the Forensic Science Society* 25, 3 (May/June 1985): 233–38.

Jora, Jürgen. *Foot Reflexology: A Visual Guide for Self-Treatment.* New York: St. Martin's, 1991.

Kahane, David, and Thorton, John. "Discussion of 'Estimating Height and Weight from Size of Footprints.'" *Journal of Forensic Sciences* 32, 1 (January 1987): 9–10.

Kramrisch, Stella. *Painted Delight: Indian Paintings from Philadelphia Collections.* Philadelphia: Philadelphia Museum of Art, 1986.

Laskowski, Gregory E. "An Improved Technique for the Visualization of Footprint Impressions in the Insoles of Athletic Shoes." *Journal of Forensic Sciences* 32, 2 (July 1987): 1075–78.

———, and Kyle, Vernon L. "Barefoot Impressions — A Preliminary Study of Identification Characteristics and Population Frequency of Their Morphological Features." *Journal of Forensic Sciences* 33, 2 (March 1988): 378–88.

*Leach, Maria. *The Luck Book.* Cleveland: World, 1964.

Levy, Howard S. *Chinese Footbinding: The History of a Curious Erotic Custom.* New York: Bell, 1967.

Lister, Margot. *Costumes of Everyday Life: An Illustrated History of Working Clothes from 900–1910.* Boston: Plays, Inc., 1972.

Lucock, L. J. "Identifying the Wearer of Worn Footwear." *Journal of the Forensic Science Society* 7, 1 (January 1967): 62–70.

Mazza, Samuele. *Cinderella's Revenge.* San Francisco: Chronicle Books, 1994.

McDowell, Colin. *Shoes: Fashion and Fantasy.* London: Thames & Hudson, 1989.

Merrifield, H. H. "Female Gait Patterns in Shoes with Different Heel Heights." *Ergonomics* 14, 3 (1971): 411–17.

*Mitchell, Barbara. *Shoes for Everyone: A Story about Jan Matzeliger.* Minneapolis: Carolrhoda Books, 1986.

Morton, Dudley J., and Fuller, Dudley Dean. *Human Locomotion and Body Form.* Baltimore: Williams & Wilkins, 1952.

Music, Doreen K., and Bodziak, William J. "Evaluation of the Air Bubbles Present in Polyurethane Shoe Outsoles as Applicable in Footwear Impression Comparisons." *Journal of Forensic Sciences* 33, 5 (September 1988): 1185–97.

Noorlander, H. *Wooden Shoes: Their Makers and Their Wearers.* Trans. Patricia Wardle. Arnheim: Netherlands Open Air Museum, 1978.

Norman, Laura. *Feet First: A Guide to Foot Reflexology.* New York: Simon & Schuster, 1988.

Norman, Scott. *How to Buy Great Shoes That Fit.* New York: Crown, 1988.

Peacock, John. *Costume 1066–1966.* London: Thames & Hudson, 1990.

Plotkin, Mark J. *Tales of a Shaman's Apprentice.* New York: Viking Penguin, 1993.

Redfern, W. B. *Royal and Historic Gloves and Shoes.* London: Methuen, 1904.

Ribeiro, Aileen, and Cumming, Valerie. *The Visual History of Costume.* London: B. T. Batsford, 1989.

Ricci, Stefania, and Maeder, Edward. *Salvatore Ferragamo: The Art of the Shoe 1898–1960.* New York: Rizzoli, 1992.

Robbins, Louise M. "Estimating Height and Weight from Size of Footprints." *Journal of Forensic Sciences* 31, 1 (January 1986): 143–52.

Roberts, M. Glenn. "Bound in Beauty: Chinese Footbinding." *Lady's Gallery,* April/May 1995.

Rowe, W. F. "Interpretation of Shoe Wear Patterns in a Personal Injury Case." *Journal of Forensic Sciences* 26, 3 (July 1981): 608–11.

Sebesta, Judith Lynn, and Bonfante, Larissa, eds. *The World of Roman Costume.* Madison: University of Wisconsin Press, 1994.

Severn, Bill. *If the Shoe Fits.* New York: David McKay, 1964.

Sharer, Robert J. *Ancient Maya.* 5th ed. Palo Alto, Calif. Stanford University Press, 1994.

*Silverstein, Alvin, and Silverstein, Virginia B. *The Story of Your Foot.* New York: Putnam's, 1987.

Swann, June. *Shoes.* Costume Accessories series. London: B. T. Batsford, 1982.

Thompson, M. W. *Novgorod the Great.* New York: Praeger, 1967.

Trasko, Mary. *Heavenly Soles: Extraordinary Twentieth-Century Shoes.* New York: Abbeville, 1989.

Tremaine, M. David, and Awad, Elias M. *The Foot and Ankle Sourcebook.* Los Angeles: Lowell House, 1995.

The True History of Shoe Sizes. Long Island City, N.Y.: Sterling Last Corp.

VanHoven, Harvey. "A Correlation Between Shoeprint Measurements and Actual Sneaker Size." *Journal of Forensic Sciences* 30, 4 (October 1985): 1233–37.

Welch, Stuart Cary, Schimmel, Annemarie, Swietochowski, Marie L., and Thackston, Wheeler M. *The Emperors' Album: Images of Mughal India.* New York: Metropolitan Museum of Art, 1987.

Wilcox, R. Turner. *The Mode in Costume.* New York: Scribner's, 1958.

———. *The Mode in Footwear.* New York: Scribner's, 1948.

Wilford, John Noble. "Fog Thickens on Climate and Origin of Humans." *New York Times,* 17 May 1994, C1, 8.

———. "Tiny Foot Bones May Show a Giant Leap for Mankind." *New York Times,* 28 July 1995, A1, 6.

———. "The Transforming Leap, From 4 Legs to 2." *New York Times,* 5 September 1995, C1, 9.

*Windrow, Martin, and Hook, Richard. *The Footsoldier.* Oxford, England: Oxford University Press, 1982.

Yarwood, Doreen. *The Encyclopedia of World Costume.* New York: Bonanza, 1986.

*Young, Robert. *Sneakers: The Shoes We Choose.* Minneapolis: Dillon, 1991.

Index

91